T0193360

OTHER BOOKS BY THE AUTHOR

The following titles are books by the author

*Fresh Anointing
*From Tears to Cheers
* Don't Give Up!
*Being an Uncommon Achiever
*Destined for Victory
*Fishing for Fruitfulness
*Candidate for the Throne
*Divine Enthronement
*Movement to the Next Level
*Sexual Crimes
*The Key to a Happy Home
*Changing You Story with You Act*Conquest over Frustration
*7 Habits of Highly Ineffectual People
*Changing Your Darkness to Daystars
*Understanding the Four Phases of Life
*The Potency of Your Word
*The Race, the Rehearsals, the Ring

****

PILLARS
— AND —
CATERPILLARS

Johnson F. Odesola

authorHOUSE®

AuthorHouse™
1663 Liberty Drive
Bloomington, IN 47403
www.authorhouse.com
Phone: 1 (800) 839-8640

© 2020 Johnson F. Odesola. All rights reserved.

No part of this book may be reproduced, stored in a retrieval system, or
transmitted by any means without the written permission of the author.

Published by AuthorHouse 12/18/2019

ISBN: 978-1-7283-4002-9 (sc)
ISBN: 978-1-7283-4001-2 (e)

Print information available on the last page.

Any people depicted in stock imagery provided by Getty Images are models,
and such images are being used for illustrative purposes only.
Certain stock imagery © Getty Images.

KJV
Scripture taken from The Holy Bible, King James Version. Public Domain

This book is printed on acid-free paper.

Because of the dynamic nature of the Internet, any web addresses or links contained in
this book may have changed since publication and may no longer be valid. The views
expressed in this work are solely those of the author and do not necessarily reflect the
views of the publisher, and the publisher hereby disclaims any responsibility for them.

Acknowledgement

All praise to God the Father, Jesus my Savior and the Holy Spirit the director of my life and inspiration. My sincere appreciation to Bisi my wife for her unflinching support and encouragement and to my home church members, Titi, Uche and Enoch. And my special thanks to my spiritual parents Daddy and Mummy E. A. Adeboye they are both my coaches to walk with the Maker of millionaires.

Thank you all may God bless you.

Contents

Preface

Let me give you a typical example in our contemporary world. The world Trade Centre, WTC was built by great minds. The Architects, Engineers and Builders that built this historic edifice are PILLARS in the society. They are constructive, positive and a plus to the world.

However, in September 11, 2001, another group of people caused pain and sorrow to the world without a spark of pity. They brought down the World Trade Centre. These destructive and negative people constituted themselves as CATERPILLARS in the society.

The world has not ceased to nurse these two groups of people: Pillars and Caterpillars. THE CHURCH has enough of these groups of people too. My purpose of writing this book is to make as many believers as possible, world- wide, realize that they can and should be pillars in the church. How to become a pillar and the benefits of being a pillar in the church will be discussed in this volume.

Pillars are carriers. They carry the structure of a building. Pillars prevent collapse. They bear the weight of the building.

Pillars guarantee stability. They hold the entire framework together.

A brief mention of CATERPILLARS will suffice. It is irrelevant to dwell much on this negative, destructive and minus set of people. I will briefly mention their activities and then proceed to talk extensively on the PILLARS. May the Lord make you a PILLAR in the church!

Chapter One

THE NEW TESTAMENT CHURCH

Irrespective of race, color or demography, there are three groups of people on earth:

The Jews
The Gentiles
The Church

The Jews are the children of Israel; every human on earth with Jewish blood running in their veins.

The Gentiles are all other nations on earth. That is, all other nations apart from the Jews. This is referred to as the gentile world.

The Church comprises of those who are born again amongst the Jews and Gentiles. They are the called out ones; called out from the Jews and Gentile world; called out of darkness into His marvelous light.

Apostle Peter describes believers in Christ as lively stones that make up the spiritual house (the body of Christ). The body of Christ; the church is the result of the work of redemption. When Jesus died and resurrected, the church was born; born to accommodate all those who call upon His name, whether Jews or Gentiles.

'Ye also, as lively stones, are built up a spiritual house, an holy priesthood, to offer up spiritual sacrifices, acceptable to God by Jesus Christ'- 1Peter 2:5.

The church is the beginning of the New Testament. The blood of Jesus was the price; the foundation and the basis of her existence. When Peter made that great revelation of Jesus being the Christ, the son of the living God, Jesus made a resounding statement in Matthew 16:18

'And I say also unto thee, That thou art Peter, and upon this rock I will build my church; and the gates of hell shall not prevail against it'.

Upon this rock: the revelation of Christ, the son of the living God, I will build my church. Jesus is the eternal Rock of ages. He is the Stone rejected by earthly, carnal, religious and degenerate builders.

'Wherefore also it is contained in the scripture, Behold, I lay in Sion a chief corner stone, elect, precious: and he that believeth on him shall not be confounded'- 1 Peter 2:6

The Rock is Jesus Christ. He that believes in Him shall not be confounded. Referring to the Eternal Rock upon which the church is built, Apostle Paul made a succinct declaration and revelation: ... *and that Rock was Christ!* - 1 Cor. 10:4

Now, the church is not meant to be subdued but to dominate from coast to coast and sea to sea. The gates of hell shall not prevent, stop, hinder or prevail over the church. Let me acquaint you with some glorious revelations about the church of Jesus Christ:

THE CHURCH is the hope of this depraved, degenerate and despicable world. Jesus Christ in the church and head of the church is our hope of glory. The world will know the benefit of the church when she is taken away in rapture. Then the wickedness, horror and terror of the devil will be unlimited and unrestricted.

THE CHURCH is the voice of God to man and the voice of man to God. Saddled with the ministry of reconciliation, she has the responsibility of talking to God for man (prayer) and talking to man for God (evangelism).

THE CHURCH is the light of the world and salt of the earth. She is a beacon of light to the benighted. Her primary duty is to let her light so shine before men that they might see her good works and glorify God. She is to take away the bitterness of the world by her saltiness.

THE CHURCH is empowered to stop the devil. As Jesus was anointed with the Holy Ghost and power to deliver those oppressed by the devil, so is the church anointed to bring healing, deliverance and restoration to mankind.

THE CHURCH is the source of solace to the confused world of spiritual blind, barren and bankrupt mortals. She is the hope of the hopeless and help of the helpless. She disseminates the joy of the Lord to cancel the sadness of a prodigal world.

THE CHURCH is the custodian of the truth that sets free. FREEDOM is the pertinent need of the world. The word of God is the basic tool of freedom. This is the greatest asset bequeathed to her.

THE CHURCH is a kingdom of priests! The New Testament believer is a priest. We are royal priesthood. The priest functions primarily to mediate between God and man. That's who the church is: mediator. The world will be lost forever without the church.

I have taken time and space to reveal God's purpose for the church in order to lay a solid foundation upon which the message of PILLARS will be built. The church exists to fulfill divine mandate. God did not place the church on earth only to clamor for and receive mundane blessings.

If the aforementioned purposes of the church are not relevant, then the church is not relevant on earth. Believers in Christ should simply die as soon as they get saved! The church exists to fulfill divine purpose.

<u>We are saved to serve. As a living organism, the church is expected to row spiritually, numerically and financially.</u> The church is supposed to grow in leaps and bounds, from coast to coast and influence the state. The church exists to save the lost at all cost.

In life generally, there are two extreme categories of people. The two groups or categories are like parallel lines that can never meet. The status of any organization, state or church depends largely on which of the categories wields enormous power and influence:

There are constructive and destructive people. There are positive and negative people.

There are plus and minus people.

CHARACTERISTICS OF CATERPILLARS

They crawl in and out of church without specific positive input. They are merely bench warmers, never active and ever passive.

They are the Far-I-See (Pharisees), always seeing far away from the truth and never seeing closely to play a supportive role in church.

They are the Sad-you-see (Sadducees), only seeing the sad side of things. They never see the good and positive sides.

They are the rumor mongers and backbiters.

They are divisive in their dispositions and mannerism.

They are perpetual late comers and like Jonah, always sleep in church. They are noise and trouble makers.

They are always negatively controversial.

They are the doubting Thomas, always seeing impossibilities. They discourage others from doing the right things in church. They sow seeds of discord in the church.

They are perpetual critics

They are always sarcastic, cynical and bigoted. They are carnally minded.

They are self-centered.

They are proud and haughty.

They are always indifferent to the things of God. They are spiritually frivolous and indolent.

Chapter Two

PILLARS IN CHURCH

There are PILLARS in the Church. The phenomenal growth of the church spiritually, numerically and financially is the result of their positive activities and input. There are two principal aspects of the church: GROWTH and HEALTH. A healthy church grows just like a healthy human grows. When a church is healthy, her spiritual, numerical and financial growth is inevitable. PILLARS are behind church health and growth.

'And when James, Cephas, and John, who seemed to be pillars, perceived the grace that was given unto me, they gave to me and Barnabas the right hands of fellowship; that we should go unto the heathen, and they unto the circumcision'- Gal.2:9

Are you a pillar or caterpillar? You will do well to check up yourself in the mirror of the next chapter of this book that outlines and deals with characteristics of pillars. If you are bankrupt of these features, it is an indication that you are a caterpillar. And if you are a caterpillar, there is an opportunity for you to become a pillar. Chapter three deals with this aspect. May the Lord make you a PILLAR in the church!

CHARACTERISTICS OF PILLARS

1: Pillars Have Genuine Encounter with God

The starting point of becoming a pillar in the church is salvation. Pillars preeminently have a genuine encounter with God. Genuine encounter is not fast and pray and still be a prey to the devil.

Genuine encounter with God is not being churchy. Several people are merely religious and churchy. The real encounter I am talking about is not 'churchianity' but 'Christianity'. Are you a genuine Christian? A young man was asked whether he was a Christian. His reply was both startling and impressive. He answered: go and ask my neighbors.

Can your neighbors say that you are a Christian? Can they follow your steps and take your counsel? Someone once boasted, 'if this person says she is a Christian and enters heaven, as a witch, I will enter heaven too and my fellow witches will make it to heaven'. This is a serious indictment!

Are you genuinely born again? Do you merely bear a Christian name? Are you merely a son or daughter of genuinely converted Christian parents? Is it because you are a choir member that makes you think you are a genuine Christian?

Until you have a genuine encounter with God, you cannot be a pillar in the church. Pillars are genuinely born again. It reflects in their lifestyles and dispositions. This genuine encounter is demonstrated in their motives, choices, character, conversations, pursuits and devotion. Their words, thoughts and actions reveal this transformed nature.

This has nothing to do with positions, status or titles in church. There are pastors and workers who are not genuinely born again. In fact, there are self- styled prophets, evangelists, teachers and apostles who do not have their names written in the book of life.

'Nevertheless the foundation of God standeth sure, having this seal, The Lord knoweth them that are his. And, Let everyone that nameth the name of Christ depart from iniquity'- 2 Tim.2:19

The Lord knows those who are genuinely born again. He knows those who are actually caterpillars but pretend to be pillars. If you are in this category, you become a pillar. 'Therefore if any man be in Christ, he is a new creature: old things are passed away; behold, all things are become new'- 2 Cor. 5:17

Pillars demonstrate a new life in Christ. They are new creatures who no longer live according to the dictates of the world and the flesh. Their yea is yea and their nay is nay. They are candid, sincere and truthful. They live in newness of Christ.

Pillars have their flesh mortified. Their affections are on things above and not on earth. They are pilgrims on a journey to meet the REDEEMER. They walk in Christ, deeply rooted and built up in him. Christ is their hope of glory. In Him they live, move and have their being.

'As ye have therefore received Christ Jesus the Lord, so walk ye in him: Rooted and built up in him, and stablished in the faith, as ye have been taught, abounding therein with thanksgiving- Col.2:6-7

<u>Pillars have genuine depth in Christ. They are not shallow like the nominal, noxious and niggard church goers who merely warm the bench Sunday after Sunday.</u> They take their root downward and bear their fruits upward.

The church was just five minutes away from starting. It was a bright Sunday morning. As usual, the regular members would arrive early to occupy their seats. This Sunday was not different. The hall was pretty full to capacity. All hands were on deck to get the service started: the choir, ushers, protocol and other departmental personnel were properly positioned.

Suddenly there was commotion from one end of the auditorium. There were all kinds of noise, giggling and howling. This was followed by shrills, cries and shouts of pain and of people tippling over one another. Seats were clattering and breaking. Then suddenly there appeared the cause of the commotion. The devil himself, identified with a shout by one of the ushers. He was clad in black attire with horns on his head and deadly clubs in his filthy hands. His appearance was very scary. Of course everybody, including the pastor ran away but one elderly man sat unperturbed in the front seat. He sat tight on his seat in defiance. The devil was mad and went straight to accost him:

Devil: "So you are the only one who is not afraid of me? Elderly man (Pillar): "Yes, I am not.

Devil: "I am the devil."

Elderly man (Pillar): "I know!"

Devil: "You know? And how dare you sit down there, daring me?"

Elderly man (Pillar): "Well it is because I am familiar with your ways having lived with your sister for twenty five years and I am still living with her."

Devil: "Good!" the devil quipped "So how were you able to cope with my sister for so long?"

Elderly man (Pillar): "I am under the authority of Christ, so I have authority over the devil and all those associated with him". The devil quietly departed from the man and the premises.

Only pillars that have genuine encounter with God can have this kind of boldness and authority. The devil flees when they resist him. They are strong in the Lord and in the power of his might having preeminently put on the whole amour of God

2: Pillars Are Sheep, Not Goats

The church has both sheep and goats.

'When the Son of man shall come in his glory, and all the holy angels with him, then shall he sit upon the throne of his glory: And before him shall be gathered all nations: and he shall separate them one from another, as a shepherd divideth his sheep from the goats: And he shall set the sheep on his right hand, but the goats on the left'- Matt.25: 31-33 The teachings and instructions of Jesus were tinctured with parables and examples. One of such was the separation of the sheep from the goats in the final judgment. It is akin to the parable of the wheat and tares. Both the wheat and tares were required to grow together until the day of reckoning. Read details in Matt. 13:24-29

In the church, the sheep and goats mingle together. They attend church services together. They have the same leadership over them. They hear the same sermons week after week. The difference between them is in their actions and reactions.

Sheep are compliant and obedient. Naturally, when you chase away a sheep from a certain spot once, he goes away and never comes back there. With a goat, you would have to do so over and over until you remove the valuable you are preserving.

The book of John chapter ten gives us vivid attributes of the sheep. Pillars are sheep, caterpillars are goats. As sheep, pillars have the following attitudes:

1. They Have A Shepherd

It is their nature to follow the instructions of the leader. They fast and pray when it is scheduled to take place by leadership. They obey the leadership to undertake evangelism and visitation. They stay under the authority of leadership, not defiant and rebellious like goats. *'But he that entereth in by the door is the shepherd of the sheep'*- John 10:2

2. They Know the Voice of the Shepherd

There are several imposing voices all over the society in which we live. Some of them are compelling and others are alluring. As sheep, pillars decipher and discern accurately the voice of the shepherd. Pillars are able to listen to the voice of constituted authority and act accordingly. *'I am the good shepherd, and know my sheep, and am known of mine'*- John 10:14.3. They Follow the Shepherd

Pillars follow the examples and dictates of leadership. They do not criticize leadership or take instructions for granted. They follow instructions step after step. And they are fanatical about this! They trust their leadership enough to follow them sheepishly and take their orders hook-line-sinker. Like father, like son. This is true of pillars. They are like their leader in godly characters and disposition. *'And when he putteth forth his own sheep, he goeth before them, and the sheep follow him: for they know his voice'*- John 10:4

4. They Do Not Listen To the Voice of the Hireling

It is obvious that there are hirelings all over the nations of the earth. Pillars are mature spiritually to resist the voice of strangers. They are not like children tossed to and fro by every wind of doctrine. They are strong in the Lord and in the power of his might.

'And a stranger will they not follow, but will flee from him: for they know not the voice of strangers' John 10:5.

#3: Pillars Are Loyal To God and Constituted Authority

One of the virtues of good followership is loyalty. Pillars are loyal to God and constituted authority. The Bible is dotted with examples of pillars who were loyal to leadership. Elisha was a pillar in Elijah's ministry. His loyalty spanned from Gilgal to Bethel, Jericho and Jordan. He served his master with absolute loyalty. Joshua was loyal to Moses. He served diligently throughout the ministry of Moses. His loyalty took him as far as becoming the leader that eventually led the children of Israel to the land of promise.

A prominent place is carved out for leadership in the bible. Absolute loyalty is required of the followership. Pillars understand this leadership-followership demand. That is why they are loyal. *'And they rose early in the morning, and went forth into the wilderness of Tekoa: and as they went forth, Jehoshaphat stood and said, Hear me, O Judah, and ye inhabitants of Jerusalem; Believe in the LORD your God, so shall ye be established; believe his prophets, so shall ye prosper'*- 2 Chron. 20:20

Having instructed Jehoshaphat how to handle and defeat the allied forces of Ammon, Moab and Mount Seir, he told him to tell the children of Israel to 'Believe in the LORD your God, so ye shall be established; believe his prophets, so ye shall PROSPER'.

God is a God of order. He has set leadership in place to cater for his people. Your pastor or whoever is the head of your church or ministry has spiritual oversight of the congregation. As there is hierarchy in physical authority, there is hierarchy in spiritual authority. If you do not believe and honour him, you will not benefit from his spiritual authority. If you despise your prophet, you will forfeit your progress.

'He that receiveth a prophet in the name of a prophet shall receive a prophet's reward; and he that receiveth a righteous man in the name of a righteous man shall receive a righteous man's reward'- Matt. 10:42

Your pastor or spiritual leader is God's representative. How you treat him determines how God will treat you. Your loyalty to him makes you a pillar in the ministry or church he leads. God says you will prosper if you believe in your pastor. The ball is in your court. You can fast and pray for prosperity but taking care of and being loyal to your spiritual leader is a cheaper and quicker option. The choice is exclusively yours!

A pillar in church that is loyal can be compared to a good ambassador. An ambassador does not reflect his own ideas or visions but only those of his home country. A loyal pillar does not reflect his own vision but that of his spiritual leader.

A loyal pillar can also be likened to a good wife. A good wife obeys instructions and genuinely supports her husband. She recognizes her husband asher head and leader. She is not independent and difficult to control. This is how a pillar is. He or she is like a good wife, obedient, compliant, supportive and absolutely loyal.

In these days of proliferation of churches and ministries, there is also a proliferation of disloyal associates like Absalom, Adonijah, Ahitophel, Shemei, Joab and Judas.

How do you know a loyal person in leadership?

In order to avoid gender repetitions, let's use the masculine pronoun, he, and possessive pronoun, his, to represent both males and females:

He is protective of his pastor, always prepared to shield him against any problems arising from his mistakes.

He is not envious of his pastor's position.

He readily gives wise counsels and good ideas to move the church forward. He acquires his pastor's tapes and books in order to benefit more from his anointing.

He uses his pastor as a good example when he speaks or preaches. He blesses his pastor with gifts.

He flows with policies and decisions made by his pastor even if there are better options.

He sees off his pastor when he is travelling and waits at the airport to welcome him when he comes back.

He regards his association with his pastor as a learning process. He makes sure everything is well with his pastor.

He refuses to take praise for great happenings but refers to his pastor as his mentor from whom he received wisdom to perform well.

He genuinely honors his pastor.

He talks about his pastor positively always.

He quotes his pastor in order to drive home his point. He goes extra miles to make his pastor happy.

#4: Pillars Are Reliable and Dependable

Naturally, you can lean on the pillars that sustain an edifice. There is no fear of possible collapse. This is how pillars in the church are. They are reliable and dependable.

There are brethren who cannot be relied on. They are not dependable. If you cast your precious pearls to their hands, they will destroy both you and your pearls. They cannot be trusted. There are hidden strains of deceit in their hearts.

Judas is chief in this line of deception. He betrayed the Lord with a kiss. Peter boasted that he will go all the way with Jesus. He even attempted to defend Jesus by pulling out his sword to cut off the servant of the high priest's ear. But when the chips were down and reality dawned on him that his master would be arrested and prosecuted, he reclined and denied ever knowing him.

Pillars are reliable. They are not betrayers like Judas. They are dependable and not fair weather Christians like Peter. When Jesus was finally taken away to Pilate, all his disciples deserted him. They were too scared to identify with him.

Pillars are always ready to go all the way with their leader. They are there when it is rosy or thorny. They are there in good and bad times. They are like central bank; a render of last resort. When it is dark and dreary, bleak and black, boisterous and stormy, they stand with the leadership like the rock of Gibraltar.

Apostle Paul had such pillars around him. He had Epaphras who was always laboring with him to uphold the Colossian church. He had pillars like Epaphroditus, Timothy, Clement, Priscilla and others. These men and women were with him through thick and thin to make full proof of his ministry.

When a person is reliable and dependable: He keeps vital information.

He is always handy.

His duty post is never deserted. He covers loopholes.

He shields his leader from ridicule. He is ever ready to serve.

He is always available at the nick of time.

He gives objective reports like Joseph to his father. He reports rebellion to leadership like Mordecai.

He creates bridges to prevent his leader from falling into pits. He takes blames in lieu of his leader.

He shares the burdens of his leader

He acts like Uzzah who held the Ark from toppling.

#5: Pillars Are Dutiful

One of the greatest virtues of pillars is that they are very dutiful. They have a sense of responsibility. There is a certain mentality that is peculiar to them. I call this OWNER'S MENTALITY or STAKEHOLDERS MENTALITY. Someone who has this kind of mentality takes the job, business or church as his own. He handles the organization as his own and so does things with great diligence.

Pillars with owner's mentality have the same kind of zeal like the founder. Let me explain this using the bank as an example. Those who work in the bank are not necessarily called bankers. The cashier, Teller, Manager etc. They work in the bank and so are bank workers. They receive their wages and other incentives every month.

Now, if there is any problem that confronts the bank like government policies, liquidity issues or other forms of setbacks, the cashier or Teller have nothing to worry about. They are only bank workers. They are not the owners of the bank. They are not major stakeholders.

The bank Directors and chairman however will handle matters differently. They will not sit and fold their arms like the cashiers and tellers who are employees of the bank. The chairman and directors are the bank owners. They are the real bankers. They are the real stakeholders. Their thinking and agitations are always different from other workers.

When an employee thinks like the Director or Chairman, gets worried and agitated and does something to solve the problems the bank is facing, then, he has the owner's mentality. He has the stakeholder's mentality. He may not necessarily become a director but he has the owner's mentality.

This is true of pillars in the church. They have the founder's or pastor's mentality. They are as dutiful, zealous and concerned as the founder or head of the church: regional, zonal or parish.

Pillars are efficient and effective. They are productive in all ramifications. When they are given any assignment, count it done. They are good finishers of what they start. Are you a pillar? You should seek to be one if you are not.

Pillars run with the vision. Rather than walk or crawl with assignments, they run with them. Their sole goal is to fulfill and accomplish the job. They do not give excuses or reasons why it is impossible to accomplish a task. They always do their assignments well.

6: Pillars Honor the Lord with Their Substances

Pillars honour the Lord with their substances.

'Honour the LORD with thy substance, and with the first fruits of all thine increase: So shall thy barns be filled with plenty, and thy presses shall burst out with new wine'- Prov. 3:9-10

It is not enough to claim the verse that says, 'and my God shall supply all your needs according to his riches in glory by Christ Jesus' in Philippians 4:19. You must fulfill the preceding conditions. The scripture above says your barns shall be filled with plenty, and your press shall burst out with new wine if you honor the Lord with your substance and with the first fruit of all your increase. There are three major dimensions in this regard. Pillars willingly honor the Lord with their substances thus. OFFERING

It is what you willingly give for the furtherance of the gospel of Christ. You want God to offer you prosperity? Offer Him your substance too. Pillars contribute to the development of the ministry. They give cheerfully and bountifully. They are involved in project execution. And they do not go to the house of the Lord empty. Whenever money is needed to carry out one ministry project or the other, they are readily available to make free will offerings.

FIRST FRUIT

First fruit is your first salary or profit. It is also your added profit when you are promoted. If you have a new job, your first salary is your first fruit. God wants you to honor Him with it. If you start a business and make profit, that first profit is your first fruit. And if you are promoted, for example from a salary of $1000 to $1200, the difference of $200 between your old and new salary is the first fruit of your increase. Pillars freely and cheerfully give their first fruit without hesitation. They know it belongs to God. Do you believe the scriptures and comply with this principle of first fruit?

TITHE

Tithe is the tenth part or 10% of your salary or profit if you are a businessman. It belongs to God. It is your seed. Pillars regularly, correctly and cheerfully give their tithes. They do not hold back this portion of their substances. Caterpillars rob God of this portion.

'Will a man rob God? Yet ye have robbed me. But ye say, Wherein have we robbed thee? In tithes and offerings. Ye are cursed with a curse: for ye have robbed me, even this whole nation. Bring ye all the tithes into the storehouse, that there may be meat in mine house, and prove me now herewith, saith the LORD of hosts, if I will not open you the windows of heaven, and pour you outa blessing, that there shall not be room enough to receive it. And I will rebuke the devourer for your sakes, and he shall not destroy the fruits of your ground; neither shall your vine cast her fruit before the time in the field, saith the LORD of hosts'- Mal. 3:8-10

Pillars honour the Lord with their time, talent and treasures

TIME

Pillars invest their time for and in God. They are always available to honor the Lord with their time because they understand that time is preeminently a gift from God. They know God is the sole owner of time and so they give Him as much as He requires. They carve out time to fast and pray. They create time to evangelize and do visitation. The make time to attend church services and programs.

TALENT

Pillars use their talents to please the Lord and bless the church. They do not hoard their God-given talents and endowments. They are committed to God and offer themselves to be maximally used of God. They cheerfully offer their skills and abilities to promote the kingdom. They serve God with their beauty, voice, writing skills, eloquence, physical muscles and whatever endowments they possess.

TREASURE

Pillars know that silver and gold belong to God. They know that their money is the connecting rod to the treasury of God. So, they spend carelessly for God. They are like Apostle Paul who said: *'And I will very gladly spend and be spent for you…'* - 2 Cor. 12:15

There is a story of two people who went to God for apple seed. Their purpose is to plant the seeds and have constant supply of apple. So, God gave them apple seeds. Two of them planted the apple seeds. One of them went further to do other post planting services such as watering, weeding, pruning and the rest. The other hindered all these natural processes.

At the fullness of time, the one who took care of his field started to harvest apple fruits while the other had nothing to harvest. When he went back to God to complain, God said to him: you hindered nature and the principles of crop production.

I vividly remember the story of my encounter with a man of God in 1977. It was in our missionary headquarters in Ibadan. My salary at that time was N140. I bought a Suzuki motor bike with N85 out of my one month salary. I was a site engineer.

One Sunday morning, I mistakenly put the envelope that contained my salary in my pocket. It was a wonderful experience. The preacher that Sunday morning was a wonderful man of God as well. During the course of his ministration, he suddenly said: 'Thus says the Lord, drop everything in your pocket in the offering bag'. I stood up almost immediately but involuntarily and shouted: 'I rebuke the devil in Jesus name!'

I did not know that how it happened but it must have been an instant reaction to the declaration of the man of God. The preacher said again in a succinct way: I- repeat, e-v-e-r-y thing in y-o-u-r p-o-c-k-e-t, bring-it-here! One of the SATGO who is now in Cameroon was in that service.

Cleverly, I took some money out of the envelope into my other pocket and went out with the remainder in the envelope to obey the declaration of the man of God. I clearly remember the song we sang in those days which we sang that memorable Sunday morning:

'As the joy of the Lord is bubbling in my heart, I will give you all my money
My money to the glory of God
My money for the glory of GodI will give you all my money

As people sang and danced out to drop all their money, I also sang but a different version; my own version. I sang it quietly in my heart as I danced out to give. This was my version of the song:

As the joy of the Lord is bubbling in my heart
I cannot give you all my money
I will go home with my transportation money
I cannot give you all my money

Whether the man of God knew that I cleverly and smartly shoved some naira notes out of the envelope, I cannot tell. But he said again with a stern voice:

'The Spirit of God just told me that some of you are disobedient. Bring everything in your pocket here now!'

Again, I played a smart one. I divided the money I initially took out of the envelope into two, put back half in the envelope and left the other half in the pocket. I was not the only one in this deception. When the man of God insisted that everything be brought to the altar, I said to myself: 'what brought me to church today? Why did I forget to leave the envelope at home?

We sang the popular 'Abraham's blessings are mine' song. And then he thundered again: 'for the last time, bring everything out here now!' That was indeed the last straw that broke the Carmel's back. I grudgingly and angrily took all the money from my pocket and gave it.

That same month, I had so much money that was more than enough.

I bought another motor bike. The money I received was N1, 978. Isn't this wonderful and rewarding? You cannot out-give God. I challenge you therefore to serve God as a pillar. It is extremely rewarding.

#7: Pillars Are Not Barriers, Barren or Bankrupt

Pillars reproduce themselves. The church that flourishes certainly has plenty of pillars. Like begets like. Pillars are spiritual giants. They are not barriers, barren or bankrupt of ideas. Their contributions to prevailing issues are always productive.

Henry Ford once said: 'My best friend is the one who can bring out the best in me'. Pillars bring out the best in people to make the church flourish. They are motivators and encouragers. They cultivate healthy relationships. There are different kinds of people

There are little minds There are average minds There are great minds

Little minds talk about people Average minds talk about things Great minds talk about ideas

Pillars are great minds

They make several valuable inputs. They are not like caterpillars who are detractors, pessimistic and mental cum spiritual pygmies. If you associate with caterpillars, they will assassinate your dreams. They are like reducing agents. Their impact always brings about reduction and division.

Pillars are 'adders' and 'multipliers'

They add value and strength to you. They multiply your worth and status. Their impact in church is exponential. They are the front liners. They are the early birds, always punctual, faithful, available and teachable.

Without vision, people perish. But without people, the vision perishes. Let me show you the strata:

1. God gives vision
2. He brings people to the vision
3. He puts the vision in the people
4. The envisioned people run with the vision. When God gives vision, the next prayer is for Him to bring the right people; pillars and

not caterpillars. If caterpillars come close to the vision, they will destroy it. They will suppress or make it drag. It is pillars that make a vision work. So, God gives the vision, brings pillars to the vision, envisions the pillars and then empowers the pillars to run with the vision.

'The Lord gave the word: great was the company of those that published it'-

Psalms 68:11.

The great company that pushes the word to win the world for the Lord is the company of pillars. They are energetic, dynamic, productive and resourceful. They are carriers of the grace and gift of God. They are valuable instruments in the hand of God.

#8: Pillars Seek His Ways, Not His Acts

People go to church for different reasons. Some people go to church to seek solutions to their problems. Others are attracted by music. Whatever brings people to church is not bad but when people do get to church, they should learn to have the right motives. This is the essence of having a genuine encounter with God.

In His earthly ministry, Jesus prospered tremendously. God anointed Him with the Holy Ghost and power. With this anointing, He went about doing good and healing all those who were sick or possessed with demons. He did not lack the power of God. His prosperity in the area of anointing was obvious to all and sundry.

One day, He demonstrated His prosperity to wipe away hunger from several thousands of people. People had followed Him for three days excitedly for the miracles, signs and wonders he was doing. They were extremely blessed too for his soul-searching messages. For three days running, they had not eaten and it was in the wilderness! Prosperity has no boundaries. Jesus took five loaves and two fishes and multiplied them to feed five thousand men apart from women and children. You know, women and children are always more in a religious gathering. Check the population of women and children in churches, fellowship centers or crusades. You will find out that they are always more in number. So, when the bible says that Jesus fed five thousand men, the number of people in the crusade was certainly more. They all fed on bread and fish to their satisfaction to the extent that twelve baskets were gathered as left over (Matthew 14:20, 21)

The situation is the same today. People go to church to have their needs me. And these needs vary.

Good husband
Faithful wife
Business connections
Miracles Healing Money
Deliverance, etc.

'The day following, when the people which stood on the other side of the sea saw that there was none other boat there, save that one whereinto his disciples were entered, and that Jesus went not with his disciples into the boat, but that his disciples were gone away alone; (Howbeit there came other boats from Tiberias nigh unto the place where they did eat bread, after that the Lord had given thanks:) When the people therefore saw that Jesus was not there, neither his disciples, they also took shipping, and came to Capernaum, seeking for Jesus. And when they had found him on the other side of the sea, they said unto him, Rabbi, when camest thou hither? Jesus answered them and said, Verily, verily, I say unto you, Ye seek me, not because ye saw the miracles, but because ye did eat of the loaves, and were filled. Labour not for the meat whichperisheth, but for that meat which endureth unto everlasting life, which the Son of man shall give unto you: for him hath God the Father sealed'- John 6: 22-27

The multitude of people that sought after Jesus were looking for bread and fish. That was what He told them. Most people seek His ACTS, only a few seek His WAYS. The ACTS of God are His blessings, provisions, miracles, healing and others. The WAYS of God are His Glory, Presence, Anointing.

Pillars seek His ways and not His acts. They seek first the kingdom of God and His righteousness. Rather than crave for miracles, they seek the Miraculous. Instead of going to church for healing, they seek the Healer. Rather than run for deliverance, they run after the Deliverer. They desire the Provider and not merely provisions. They are God chasers and not gold diggers.

Jesus did not mince his words. He was pomp and plain. He told those who sought after Him: '*Verily, verily, I say unto you, Ye seek me, not because ye saw the miracles, but because ye did eat of the loaves, and were filled.*

This is the pathetic condition of some people. They are in church for only what they can get from God. To them, God is like Father Christmas. They are always at the receiving end, always collecting and never giving. Is this your style? Are you seeking God for what you can get from Him?

The advice Jesus gave to the people is what I will reiterate too to those who are after God for only mundane blessings which are merely tangible, transient and ephemeral:

Labour not for the meat which perisheth, but for that meat which endureth unto everlasting life, which the Son of man shall give unto you: for him hath God the Father sealed'

Seek to be pillars in the house of God by going after the Miraculous, Healer, Provider and Deliverer. Go after God and not his gold. You can be a pillar in the church. You can get out of the comfort zone of seeking His acts and get engrossed with the desire for His ways: His glory and presence. Brethren, time has come for us to remain strong for the Lord as pillars. Let us do away with this bread and butter kind of churchianity. Let our affection be on things above and not on earthly things. Let it be what you can do for the Lord and not what the Lord should do for you.

God is looking for pillars to seek and worship Him in Spirit and in truth. Are you ready to offer yourself as one? Will you put the interest of God before your material needs? Is God your primary desire? You have the chance of making amendment now and become a pillar in the hands of God.

'*And this they did, not as we hoped, but first gave their own selves to the Lord, and unto us by the will of God'*- 2 Cor. 8:5

'*But seek ye first the kingdom of God, and his righteousness; and all these things shall be added unto you'*- Matt. 6:33.

#9: Pillars Are Faithful

Faithfulness is a major requirement in stewardship. Pillars are faithful to God, the constituted authority and in the discharge of their responsibilities.

When it comes to faithfulness, this is where several people have issues. God is faithful. He requires us to be faithful in all ramifications.

'Moreover it is required in stewards that a man be found faithful'- 1 Cor. 4:2

'A faithful man shall abound with blessings: but he that maketh haste to be rich shall not be innocent'- Prov. 28:20

There are three kinds or levels of faithfulness. Faithfulness in little things.

Faithfulness in another man's business. Faithfulness in money. Faithfulness in Little Things Faithfulness is central to godly service. It begins with little things. No one will commit great responsibilities to your hands if you cannot handle little things faithfully. If N100, 000 makes you misbehave such that you abuse everyone around you, you will not get $100,000. That will make you mad. God does not want His children to end up in psychiatric hospitals.

Do you want to be a pillar in church or your organization? You must first be faithful and accountable in little things. The more faithful you are, the more you will be trusted to handle bigger things. Jesus made it clear that he that is faithful in little things will be faithful in much.

'He that is faithful in that which is least is faithful also in much: and he that is unjust in the least is unjust also in much'- Luke 16:10

Your character is an indication you will be able to handle greater things if you are given little things to handle. Some people become proud like a peacock when they are given a small responsibility. Such people cannot handle huge responsibilities. They will step on the head of people. Are you faithful? It begins with little things. Pillars are very faithful in little things.

Faithfulness in another Man's Business

If you are not faithful in another man's business, you can never be faithful with your own if you get it at all. Jacob was accountable with Laban's flocks. No wonder God blessed him. David was accountable with the sheep of his father, Jesse. No wonder God put him in charge of His sheep (Israel). Pillars are always faithful in another man's business. They are faithful with the business of the kingdom.

There are people who treat other people's business shabbily. They do not give their best service simply because it is not their own. God will not give suchpeople their own and if eventually they get it, other people will treat it shabbily. You reap what you sow; as you lay your bed, so you lie on it.

Be faithful in another man's business. This is expedient if you will prosper in your own business. Wherever you work, handle things as if they are your own. Have what I call *'owner's mentality'*. Do it as if it is yours. When you eventually have your own, you will handle it well and prosper. Jacob eventually had a large flock of animals having pre-eminently been faithful in another man's flocks.

Faithfulness in Money

Money wields so much power and influence. In some quarters, if you place God and money side by side, people will choose the latter. Money is a litmus test that differentiates pillars from caterpillars.

'...and money is a defence...'- Eccl. 7:12
'...but money answereth all things'- Eccl. 10:19

Economic power is only next to spiritual power. Money is power. It is the only thing Jesus Christ compared with God. Surely, God is incomparable. Jesus did not say that man shall not serve God and Satan. You don't need Satan in any way in life. You do need God and money. Money is indispensable as God is in life.

This is the trouble people have, especially born again Christians. They avoid fornication and adultery. They are devoted to God in fasting, prayer and bible study. They are good Christians but when it comes to money matters, their trouble begins. They are not faithful with money. That is the only *Essential* or *needful thing* they lack like the rich young lawyer. Their defence is porous with money matters.

Do you want to become a pillar for God? Can God trust you with money? You must first settle the issue of faithfulness. If you are not faithful with money, God will not commit things of eternal value to you. If you cannot handle money, it is certain you will not be able to handle anointing. Pillars are faith with little things, another man's business and money.

#10: Pillars Are Upright In Their Dispositions

'For the LORD God is a sun and shield: the LORD will give grace and glory: no good thing will he withhold from them that walk uprightly'- Psalms 84:11

No sane parent will give his treasures to a wayward, rebellious and extravagant child. God will not commit certain responsibilities to you if you are not a pillar. There is a place for righteous or upright living in the eternal plan and purpose of God. The bible says He will not withhold any good thing from those who walk uprightly.

'For thou, LORD, wilt bless the righteous; with favour wilt thou compass him as with a shield'- Psalms 5:12

Pillars are upright. As a believer, you have an obligation to live right. God will not deal with you the same way he deals with the infidel. While he requires the sinner to repent, he requires the believer to be holy. While he expects the unbeliever to believe, he expects the believer to behave. We are the righteousness of God in Christ Jesus. As we remain in his will, way and word, he will be committed to lavish his favor on us.

'The righteous shall flourish like the palm tree: he shall grow like a cedar in Lebanon'- Psalms 92:12

'Those that be planted in the house of the LORD shall flourish in the courts of our God'- Psalms 92:13

God favored and blessed Joseph because he was a formidable pillar, first in his family of orientation and then in Potiphar's house. He prospered even as a slave! One virtue that marked out Joseph was uprightness. Many young men of nowadays will sleep with Mrs. Potiphar in order to secure their job. Joseph refused to be immoral with his master's wife. This was very pleasing to God. God will acknowledge and elevate you eventually if you remain upright. Back home when he was with his siblings, he was always giving his father objective reports. He was upright in his dealings. No wonder Jacob loved him so much.

'Blessed is the man that walketh not in the counsel of the ungodly, nor

standeth in the way of sinners, nor sitteth in the seat of the scornful... and whatsoever he doeth shall prosper'- Psalms 1:1-3

God is committed to anoint and prosper those who will stay away from evil. Such people will be like a tree that is planted by the rivers of water, whose leaves shall not wither. Whatsoever they do shall prosper. Do you want to be a pillar and prosper? Be upright! Stay away from the counsel of the wicked.

Some people will multiply their evil when they have money. More money means more women. It means more clubbing and shady deals. Set your heart to live a clean and upright life. You will attract God's blessings. How responsible you are will determine the extent of God's blessings. God will rather leave you a poor fellow if prosperity will take you away from his presence like the prodigal son.

Pillars remain upright even when God prospers them stupendously. You will hardly notice any significant difference between their financially low and high points. Pride is not in their character. They are clad with humility in their conversations and dispositions.

#11: Pillars Occupy Their Priesthood

The peculiar office of a priest is to minister to God in holy things. Though there was a body of priests set apart from their brethren to offer the literal sacrifices and perform the other outward service of the tabernacle, under the New Testament scheme, every believer is a priest, set apart and consecrated to render to God spiritual service, and offer spiritual sacrifice. We are a kingdom of priests. *But ye are a chosen generation, a royal priesthood, an holy nation, a peculiar people; that ye should show forth the praises of him who hath called you out of darkness into his marvellous light'-* 1 Peter 2:9

Pillars understand and occupy their priesthood both at home and in church. They are not perpetually on the counseling line, seeking to be prayed for. They are mature, strong and vibrant. They are able to eat strong meat and bones of the bible unlike babes who are required to drink the sincere milk of the word of God.

'And hath made us kings and priests unto God and his Father; to him be glory and dominion for ever and ever. Amen'- Rev. 1:6

As a 'Royal Priesthood', every believer has a priestly ministry. The priest principally functions to offer sacrifice. Our sacrifice is three fold.

Offering of our body- Rom.12:1, 1 Cor. 6:20

Offering of the fruit of the lips- Psalms 50:23, Heb. 13:15

Offering of our substance- Heb. 13:16, Gal.6:10

Pillars know that they are kings and priests in Christ Jesus. They do not only know but occupy their position in the eternal purpose and plan of God for the church. So, they present their body as living sacrifice, offer unto God the fruit of the lips; sincere worship and thanks and of course their substance.

INTERCESSION

The New Testament believer is also an intercessor. He stands between God and man. Pillars in church understand this and take their place of intercession.

'I exhort therefore, that, first of all, supplications, prayers, intercessions, and giving of thanks, be made for all men; For kings, and for all that are in authority; that we may lead a quiet and peaceable life in all godliness and honesty'- 1 Timothy 2:1-2*'Epaphras, who is one of you, a servant of Christ, saluteth you, always labouring fervently for you in prayers, that ye may stand perfect and complete in all the will of God'*- Col.4:12

'My little children, of whom I travail in birth again until Christ be formed in you'- Gal.4:19

Pillars in the church are intercessors. They bear the burdens of ministry and soul winning with the leadership. They stand in the gap in strenuous intercession.

They talk to God for man- prayer- Eze.22:30

They talk to man for God- preaching- 11 Cor.5:11.

#12: Pillars Are Builders

We all know what pillars do. They serve as support for whatever thing for which they are used. They are useful and productive. And inversely, caterpillars are worm-like animals that crawl in and out to destroy. They are a liability to the church.

'Every wise woman buildeth her house: but the foolish plucketh it down with her hands'- Prov. 14:1

Women have always been pillars in the building of the church of Christ. They are an integral part of every successful ministry. Jesus had the support of Mary, Martha, Joana, Sussana, among others. Paul had the help of Priscilla, Aquilla's wife. Dorcas was a pillar in the days of the early church. Deborah stood to defend Israel as a rock of Gibraltar. She was a pillar in the prophetic ministry. Jael drove a nail into the temple of Sisera, captain of the host of king Jabin.

Ruth, a Moabitess took her place in the eternal plan of God. She stood vehemently with Naomi in her grievous days. In the genealogy of our Lord and Saviour, Jesus Christ, she was mentioned (Matthew 1:5). Rehab identified with the God of Israel. Though a harlot, she stood as a pillar to advance the course of God when He sent spies to Jericho in preparation for conquest. She too was mentioned in the genealogy (Matthew 1:5).

The list of women who stood as pillars goes on. You can be a pillar in your generation. Never be a caterpillar. Ask God to help you to stand with the church and ministry to be effective as a pillar. It is your turn, it is your time!

#13: Pillars Are Resolute

The messages of Jesus were hard and stern but laced with love and hope. His words were fiery, convicting and convincing. It made some wicked religious gladiators gnash their teeth. It got some people mad that they picked up stones.

In one of such soul searching messages, some of His disciples labeled his words as too hard to hear and bear. It was like a hammer that breaks rocks into pieces and sword that pierces the bones and marrows.

'Many therefore of his disciples, when they had heard this, said, This is an hard saying; who can hear it?'- John 6:60

Unlike the bread and butter messages in the lips of preachers today, the words of Jesus were coated with divine fire. They came red hot from fiery lips. They were not meant to lull the erring crowed into fatal security. His purpose was to turn the hearts of people back to God.

'From that time many of his disciples went back, and walked no more with him'- John 6:66

The congregation in this instance was his disciples. He was not preaching a simple message of salvation. His message was centered on real commitment and devotion to God. It was an invitation to become a pillar for God. You will discover this reality if you read the entire chapter six of the book of John.

> Many of his disciples went away from him. They could not come to terms with his message. They were strong meat and bones, not the usual milk that preachers pour in feeding bottles for adults to consume today. It was unbearable. *'Then said Jesus unto the twelve, Will ye also go away?'*- John 6:67

The question was straight and firm. It was pomp, plain and pointed. There was no mincing of words. The ball was thrown in the court of the remaining disciples. It was their prerogative to decide. And the question was not rhetorical. Jesus demanded instant answer.

'Then Simon Peter answered him, Lord, to whom shall we go? thou hast the words of eternal life. And we believe and are sure that thou art that Christ, the Son of the living God'- John 6:68-69

Their answer was a perfect one. They were resolute in their decision to follow Jesus. Their conclusion was: *there is no other one like you Lord, you are the only hope. There is no going back, we have decided to follow you all the way'*.

Pillars have this kind of resolve. They are resolute in their commitment. Their faces are set like a flint. Nothing can deter them. It is Jesus only, Jesus ever. They have their minds made up, having said goodbye to the world. The following lines of a popular song is true of pillars:

'I have decided to follow Jesus, I have decided to follow Jesus,
I have decided to follow Jesus,
No turning back, no turning back.

Let me ask you firmly: have you resolved to follow Jesus all the way, come what may? If no one joins you, will you still follow Jesus? Will you be satisfied with Jesus if the whole world is taken away from you?

#14: Pillars Are Submissive

> Jesus was the PILLAR of redemption. He is raising pillars for His church today. Left alone to bear the burden of redemption, he prayed earnestly in the Garden of Gethsemane. Each time he came over to check on his disciples, he met them asleep. Their eyes were heavy with sleep. He had told them to pray along with him: *'Then saith he unto them, My soul is exceeding sorrowful, even unto death: tarry ye here, and watch with me'*- Matt. 26:38

They could not tarry with him in prayer. Though willing, their flesh was weak. The hope of redemption was at stake. It rested only in one person: Jesus. It would be dashed forever unless he submitted his will. The host of heaven watched keenly as he took an eternal decision. His decision would either make or mar humanity.

'And he went a little farther, and fell on his face, and prayed, saying, O my Father, if it be possible, let this cup pass from me: nevertheless not as I will, but as thou wilt'- Matt. 26:39

Jesus was submissive. His will was lost and swallowed up in the will of Abba Father. He yielded himself totally to the will and plan of God. He would rather save man than hold on to his legitimate will.

Pillars are thus submissive. They submit to God and constituted authority. Their will becomes shadow in the presence of God. They are always ready to substitute their will for the Lord's. They are yielded and surrendered. The authority of leadership is supreme to their personal agenda. To them, it is God first, me second. Are you thus submissive to God and leadership?

#15: Pillars Are Zealous

The apostles and the early church were full of zeal. The fire of the gospel spread so rapidly in spite of persecutions and limitations placed by the religious gladiators of the day. Pentecost was the turning point. The once timid disciples went wild with the fire of zeal when the Holy Ghost descended. They were described as been drunk with wine. Indeed, they imbibed the new wine of zeal. Nothing could deter them. Nothing could quench the flames that glowed within and around them.

PILLARS are full of irrepressible and unquenchable zeal. They forge ahead with the gospel mandate in spite of oppositions. Nothing can stop them fromadvancing the course of the kingdom. They are clad with zeal as a cloak. They fan their commitment and zeal to a glowing point.

'For the zeal of thine house hath eaten me up; and the reproaches of them that reproached thee are fallen upon me'- Psalms 69:9

'And his disciples remembered that it was written, The zeal of thine house hath eaten me up'- John 2:17

'For he put on righteousness as a breastplate, and an helmet of salvation upon his head; and he put on the garments of vengeance for clothing, and was clad with zeal as a cloak'- Isaiah 59:17

Pillars are zeal personified. They are motivated by that inner glow. They are zealous in prayers, fasting, evangelism, church activities and with their assignments and responsibilities. Unlike others who are slow, slack and sluggish, fireless, frivolous and feeble, pillars are active, dynamic and vibrant. They are totally wrapped up in the cloak of His zeal.

I have stated and explained fifteen characteristics of pillars in this book. It is my earnest prayer that the Lord will make you one of his numerous pillars in this end time. You can be a pillar for God. It is God's earnest desire. Let it be your burning desire too.

Chapter Three

HOW TO BECOME A PILLAR

Pillars are not born, they are made. It is a matter of choice. While it is not for the privileged few, it is for the few who choose this privilege of being pillars. Two people can be born again the same day, hour and minute under the same preacher and message. Some years later, depending on spiritual development, one could become a pillar and the other a caterpillar.

The choice is exclusively yours to be a pillar or caterpillar. I will show you in this chapter how you can become a pillar in the church of God. Prayerfully take these steps and be sensitive and responsive in the spirit.

SURRENDER TOTALLY

'Submit yourselves therefore to God. Resist the devil, and he will flee from you'- James 4:7

Just like a tree starts to develop from the roots and grows to become a mighty living wood, becoming a pillar begins from the roots. You must have a genuine encounter with the Lord. You must be sincerely converted. A tree preeminently drives its root downward in order to grow upward.

The bane of the modern church is half baked Christians who struggle to occupy positions of authority. If you are not grounded in the words of eternal life, you cannot get people grounded. Until you are broken, you cannot break men.

Surrender totally! Be broken! The alabaster flask of oil was not useful until Mary broke it and spilled its content to anoint the feet of Jesus. It was only when it was broken that its fragrance filled the air.

Surrender totally! Be broken! The five loaves of bread and two fish were broken to feed five thousand men apart from women and children. It was a little lad's lunch. It was insufficient to feed a family. But Jesus submitted it to God with thanksgiving. Only then was it useful and sufficient.

Surrender totally! Be broken! While Jesus traversed the streets of Capernaum, Galilee and all other villages and cities he held crusades, he was geographically limited. He was in one place at a time. But after he was broken for us as offering and sacrifice, he is everywhere at the same time. He has no geographical or demographic limitations. He is ubiquitous! He is Omnipresent! Until you are surrendered and totally broken, you cannot become a pillar for God. You will amount to little in the hands of God. Only broken vessels can break men. Only men who have knelt at the cross can bring men on their knees. Are you yielded and surrendered to God and constituted authority? Are you genuinely converted?

PAY TOTAL OBEDIENCE

'If ye be willing and obedient, ye shall eat the good of the land'- Isa. 1:19
'Obedience is better than sacrifice'-

Total obedience to God and leadership will guarantee your place as a pillar for God. Disobedience is worse than witchcraft. God is not looking for witches and wizards to install as pillars in the church. Disobedience is a terrible vice, a trait of caterpillars.

Lucifer was rebellious and disobedient. He became a caterpillar afterwards. God hates disobedience. It is the character and attribute of witchcraft. You must be obedient to divine and leadership instructions in order to become a pillar.

Search yourself, how obedient are you to God and leadership? Do you grumble and murmur secretly? Do you negate the decisions and opinions of leadership? Does the spirit of Absalom have any influence on you? Are you defiant to rules and regulations?

'I will instruct thee and teach thee in the way which thou shalt go: I will guide thee with mine eye'- Psalms 32:8

The mark of pillars in the hands of God is implicit and filial obedience. Pillars are compliant to the way, word and will of God. They are swift to hear and action. They hear and act twice when God speaks once.

BE UNDER ORDER

'And having in a readiness to revenge all disobedience, when your obedience is fulfilled'- 2 Cor 10:6 You don't have authority until you are under authority. If you break the ranks, you will be useless in the hand of God. In order to be a pillar for God, you must be under order. The military institution is a perfect example of authority. Those who break ranks are made to cool off behind bars.

When you bind and cast out devils, they will obey you and leave the victim if you are obedient to authority too. The reason some people cannot handle the devil and his demons is that they are not completely under order. The seven sons of Sceva attempted to cast out demons from their victim. The consequence was humiliating. The demons rather cast them out saying: Jesus I know, Paul I know, who are you?

Are you under order? Do you break the ranks?

OFFER SINCERE SERVICE

'If they obey and serve him, they shall spend their days in prosperity, and their years in pleasures'- Job 36:11

Pillars are preeminently servants. They serve wholeheartedly. It is in the place of service that God confirms his pillars. The church is full of receivers. Only a few are givers of services. It seems to me that 20% serve the 80% of the congregation.

People come to church only to be ministered to. They receive prayers, the word, counseling, instructions, assistance, deliverance, healing. The list goes on. They are always at the collection end, never bringing anything to the table.

Where do you belong? Do you belong to the 20% who give their services or the 80% who receive? Sincere service is the ladder you must climb to become a pillar. Jesus told us that he came to serve and not to be served. His entire ministry on earth was characterized by service. He preached the gospel of salvation, healed the sick, delivered the oppressed, fed the hungry, washed people's feet and went to the cross to save mankind. What is your role in the church? Are you a receiver of giver of service? How eager are you to render your time, treasure, talent and energy to serve God and leadership? Is your service sincere and pure? People who serve should also make sure their service is pure. There are various kinds of services. God accepts only perfect services.

Lip Service: There are people that offer lip service. They are not sincere in their service. Everything about their service ends up in their lips. They offer lip worship, lip prayers and lip obedience. Their heart is never involved.

Eye Service: There are people also who offer eye service. They are active only because the pastor or leader is around. Their commitment is seen when the pastor is in sight. They serve in order to be seen by leadership. They cherish the applause and commendation of men. Their heart is not involved as well.

Heat Service: This is the kind of service that God demands of us. Those who render wholehearted service are the real pillars of the church. Their service is genuine and pure. They serve God with all their heart, mind and might.

What kind of service have you been rendering to God? Lips, eye or heart service? Is your service adulterated? Is it polluted with insincerity? Is it pure, holy and selfless? God is excellent. He will accept nothing short of excellence from you? If you desire to be a pillar, you must be ready to render sincere service to the Lord and His church.

LOVE AND SELFLESSNESS

Love is the greatest attribute of God. The bible says God is love. If you really want to be a pillar for God, love must be your greatest asset. You must be love personified. The church consists of all manners of people. Love is the virtue that will enable you to manage relationships.

'Let love be without dissimulation. Abhor that which is evil; cleave to that

which is good. Be kindly affection one to another with brotherly love; in honor preferring one another'- Rom. 12:9-10Your love for God, the leadership and the congregation must be sincere. It must not be coated with deceit. Being a pillar in the church is a huge responsibility. The church is not a jamboree center neither is it a funfair arena.

It is a place that draws on your spirit, soul and body in service. You must be ready to show love.

Love is selfless. You cannot be a pillar if you are a self-centered person. It must be JOY. Let us consider the meaning of this acronym:

J: Jesus
O: Others
Y: You

It must be Jesus first, Others second, You third. It takes selflessness to serve other people. Service is all about God and His people, not you. That is why it is Jesus first, others second and you third. Are you selfless? Some people are full of themselves. God will not make them pillars in His church.

'*...in honour preferring one another'-* Rom. 12:10

CONTENTMENT

The bible says contentment is great gain. There are people who are very covetous like Achan. Everything is about themselves. They are greedy and anxious of material things.

'For men shall be lovers of their own selves, covetous, boasters, proud, blasphemers, disobedient to parents, unthankful, unholy'- 2 Tim. 32:2

There is a wide gap between contentment and covetousness. One is a vice and the other a virtue. The contented is never covetous and the covetous is never contented. You must be contented if you desire to be a pillar for God. If you are covetous, you will not offer your substances like tithes, offerings and first fruit to the Lord. You will not be financially committed to God. *'But godliness with contentment is great gain. For we brought nothing into this world, and it is certain we can carry nothing out. And having food and raiment let us be therewith content'-* 1 Tim. 6:6-8

Checkup yourself properly and sincerely: are you covetous? Are you greedy of filthy lucre? Are you materialistic? These are the amendments you must make if you will become a pillar in the hands of God.

DYNAMIC PRAYER LIFE

Church is not a business center. It is a spiritual arena. It is not a civil realm but a spiritual terrain. You must be prayerful because the weapons of our warfare are not carnal. They are mighty and spiritual.

'(For the weapons of our warfare are not carnal, but mighty through God to the pulling down of strong holds ;). Casting down imaginations, and every high thing that exalteth itself against the knowledge of God, and bringing into captivity every thought to the obedience of Christ'- 2 Cor. 10:4-5

Lazy knees and sealed lips cannot become pillars in the church of God. You must have a dynamic prayer life. We are not contending with flesh and blood but principalities and powers. You must be ready to engage in spiritual warfare and strenuous intercessions. You must be a prayer warrior.

'And he spake a parable unto them to this end, that men ought always to pray, and not to faint'- Luke 18:1

'Pray without ceasing'

'Not slothful in business; fervent in spirit; serving the Lord'- Rom. 12:11

Prayer is a foremost requirement in stewardship. You must be given to constant payers. Prayer must be an integral part of you. If you would stand before men to serve, you must kneel before God in prayers. Pillars are prayer warriors.

PASSION FOR SOULS

Soul winning is the heart beat of God. The great commission is to make disciples of all nations. God is not about to recruit people who have no passion for souls. If you desire to be a pillar, you must be passionate about soul winning.

'Go ye therefore, and teach all nations, baptizing them in the name of the

Father, and of the Son, and of the Holy Ghost: Teaching them to observe all things whatsoever I have commanded you: and, lo, I am with you always, even unto the end of the world. Amen'- Matt. 28:19-20

In the church, there are lambs and sheep. There are also goats. It is the responsibility of pillars to cater for all of them. Jesus required Peter to prove his love for him by feeding the lambs and sheep. While the goats are to be encouraged to repent, the lambs and sheep are to be developed to become strong in the Lord and in the power of his might.

The bible says to bear the infirmities of those that are weak. God expects us to be an encouragement to one another. There is the tendency of people becoming weary in the process. Pillars are handy vessels in the church of God to uphold them.

'Brethren, if a man be overtaken in a fault, ye which are spiritual, restore such a one in the spirit of meekness; considering thyself, lest thou also be tempted. Bear ye one another's burdens, and so fulfil the law of Christ'- Gal. 6:1-2

You must have a soft spot for people in your heart if you want to be a pillar. The church is about people, not tangible goods. The church does not deal in shoes and bags. We don't sell clothes or food in church. It is all about God and His people. So, you must be people oriented. You must have passion to see that righteousness prevails in the church. It must be your goal to take as many people as possible to heaven.

BE POSITIVELY MINDED

People look at things from different perspective. A person can look at the cup as half empty while another says it is half full. Though they are both correct, half empty is a negative judgment while half full is a positive one. You must learn to be positive minded with God's heritage. His people are special to him, you must not despise or treat them with supercilious demeanor.

Don't be a Pharisee who only sees the far side of things neither behave like a Sadducee who only see the sad side of things. Be optimistic about the people you are surrounded with. See the good sides of people. Avoid unnecessary criticism and bickering. Speak well of people. Cherish relationships like jewel and be a builder and not destroyer. If you want to be a pillar, you must be positively minded.

TOLERANCE

Tolerate people. This is a compulsory virtue. You are not dealing with animals in church. The church is God's precious ones for whom Jesus died. They have been purchased by the blood of Jesus. You must tolerate people and help them to grow.

God does not cast his children away when they err. You must be ready to tolerate and accommodate people irrespective of their attitudes and dispositions. God is patient with us. Be patient with his people. They will improve even if they are slow in learning. Your job is to pray for them and counsel them as occasion demands.

These are some necessary steps you must take if you truly desire to be a pillar in the church of God. It is my earnest prayer for God to use you as his treasure; his vessel and pillar. It may look cumbersome and demanding. Rejoice for great are your rewards. God has not called us to serve in vain. He will certainly reward us accordingly.

Chapter Four

BENEFITS OF BEING A PILLAR

God is not an austere God according to the lazy submission of the servant who was given one pound in the parable Jesus gave about a noble man. God is rather magnanimous. We are all beneficiaries of his largesse. His rewards far outweigh our labour.

'For our light affliction, which is but for a moment, worketh for us a far more exceeding and eternal weight of glory'- 2 Cor. 4:17

The reward for our services as pillars is unimaginable. The bible describes it as far more exceeding and eternal weight of glory. It is inexhaustible. All our efforts in fasting and prayer, giving and supports, evangelism and visitation, counseling and exhortation are reckoned as light affliction compared to the rewards that await us in eternity.

'For I reckon that the sufferings of this present time are not worthy to be compared with the glory which shall be revealed in us'- Rom. 8:18

Apostle Paul reiterated this to the Romans and by extension to us. Let us even reckon our labour as suffering. Apostle Paul said these so called sufferings of fasting, praying, travelling all over the world to preach, giving and other efforts towards the kingdom are incomparable with the glory that God has prepared for us.

'For God is not unrighteous to forget your work and labour of love, which ye have showed toward his name, in that ye have ministered to the saints, and do minister'- Heb. 6:10Men may forget your labor of love and unflinching sacrifices. Out of the ten lepers Jesus cured, only one remembered to give

thanks. It is in the nature of men to forget the efforts of others. Man gets, gets and forgets. God gives, gives and forgives. The bible says God will never forget our efforts towards the kingdom. This is why you should labor assiduously as pillars to advance the course of the kingdom.

'Therefore, my beloved brethren, be ye stedfast, unmoveable, always abounding in the work of the Lord, forasmuch as ye know that your labour is not in vain in the Lord'-1 Cor. 15:28

God has not called us to serve in vain. He is a rewarder of those who diligently seek him. Apostle Paul enjoins us to always abound in the work of the church and ministry because our efforts will never be in vain. Having known all these, let me now summarize the benefits of being a pillar in a few points.

Prosperity and Progress: You will prosper and make meaningful progress in life if you remain a pillar. Job 36:11 says: 'If they obey and serve him, they shall spend their days in prosperity, and their years in pleasures'

DIVINE FAVOR

You will have the mercy and favor of God if you are a pillar in the kingdom. God will be favorably disposed to you. Psalms 5:12 says: 'For thou, LORD, wilt bless the righteous; with favor wilt thou compass him as with a shield'

ANSWERED PRAYER

You will receive answers to prayers with ease when you are a pillar for God. Before you call, He will hear and while you are speaking, He will answer. John 15:16 says: 'Ye have not chosen me, but I have chosen you, and ordained you, that ye should go and bring forth fruit, and that your fruit should remain: that whatsoever ye shall ask of the Father in my name, he may give it you.

ADEQUATE SECURITY

You will be adequately secured if you remain a pillar for God. The raven that God sent to give Elijah food day and night in the brook Cherith was adequately shielded from hunters. No hunter would have able to shot her down. Do you know why? She was on a mission for the Lord. If you are a pillar on a mission for the Lord, long life and health is guaranteed. God will preserve you for His purpose. Psalms 91:1, 16 says: 'He that dwelleth in the secret place of the most High shall abide under the shadow of the Almighty…With long life will I satisfy him, and show him my salvation'. You can read the entire chapter for details.

FULFILLMENT IN LIFE

There is nothing more joyful and rewarding than serving the Lord as a pillar. You will experience an inner joy of fulfillment. You will have unspeakable joy; the joy of the Lord which is our ever abiding strength.

The ball is in your court right now. I have told you the purpose of the New Testament church on earth. I have exposed you to the characteristics of pillars in the church. I have also shown you how to become a pillar for God. And finally,

I have presented to you the benefits of being a pillar. You have no excuse to be a caterpillar. This book is a witness of your knowledge of the truth. You will give account of your life someday. If you claim that you did not know about being a pillar for God, the record will be opened to show that you read this book. You are not ignorant. So, beware. Make up your mind and strive earnestly to be a pillar and not a caterpillar. God bless you.

Author's Connects

If you have been blessed by this message, you can also
contact: Pastor Johnson Funso Odesola @
Redeemed Christian Church of God Headquarters,
Ebute Mata, Lagos, Nigeria

Phone: +2348035361325; +2348074368534

Email:odesolajf@gmail.com; funsoodesola@yahoo.com
Follow me on Twitter: http://twitter.com/PastorJFOdesola
Friend me on Facebook: http://facebook.com/
PastorJFOdesola http://Youtube.com/ PastorJFOdesola
Follow me on Linkedin: http://ng,Linkedin.com/in/ PastorJFOdesola

Drop a message for me @ http://smashwords.
com/funsoodesola/profile/view

Printed in the United States
By Bookmasters